I know this to be true

NELSON MANDELA
FOUNDATION

Living the legacy

Simone Biles

I know this to be true

on family,
confidence
& persistence

Interview and photography

Geoff Blackwell

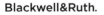

CHRONICLE BOOKS
SAN FRANCISCO

in association with

Blackwell&Ruth.

Dedicated to the legacy
and memory of
Nelson Mandela

'I'm not the next Usain Bolt or Michael Phelps. I'm the first Simone Biles.'

Introduction

When she was three years old, Simone Biles and her three siblings were placed into foster care. Their parents had a number of personal struggles and were unable to raise them alone. Because of their age, Simone and her younger sister Adria spent time in foster care, where visits from their maternal grandfather, Ron, were a consistent highlight. Finally, when she was six, he and his second wife, Nellie, legally adopted Simone and younger sister, Adria. They moved to Houston, Texas, USA, where Ron and Nellie lived with their two teenage sons, and immediately became part of the family.

It was a natural transition for Simone, who quickly took to calling her grandfather and step-grandmother 'Mom' and 'Dad'. Forming a strong bond with both parents, she received the love, generosity and stability her early years had lacked. Nellie, a nurse, was a guiding influence on Simone as she navigated childhood, offering support and kindness while instilling in her a drive and focus. Each year from the age of six, she insisted that Simone write down her short- and long-term goals, and each year they spent time together reflecting on what she had achieved. It's a practice they continue to this day.

As a six-year-old Simone began her new life in Texas and experienced her first encounter with gymnastics. During a day-care field trip to a Houston gym, she saw older girls practicing on the beam and the trampoline. An active child, she decided to try her hand at some moves. Her efforts didn't go unnoticed. One of the gymnastics coaches spotted her potential and sent her home with a letter to her parents suggesting she enrol in lessons. Not long after, she began a training programme at Bannon's Gymnastix, a gymnastics training gym in northwest Houston. It was the beginning of a journey that would irrevocably change her life.

Now, more than fifteen years since she took home that letter, Simone Biles is the most decorated gymnast in Gymnastics World Championship history. With twenty-five World Championship medals and four Olympic gold medals, she has been hailed as the greatest gymnast of all time.[i] But the road to success hasn't been easy. When she started out, a gruelling training regimen occupied around twenty hours each week. This, combined with schoolwork, allowed little time for anything else. Wanting to pour more energy into her sport without sacrificing her studies, Simone made the difficult decision to leave public school and begin homeschooling in 2012. This enabled her to increase her training by more than ten hours a week, but as a result she missed out on several key teenage experiences. 'I made a lot of sacrifices. I gave up all the school dances. I've never been to a prom. Never done a lot of those things that maybe most other kids were doing or wanted to do', she says. But of course, it was all worth it. 'I fell in love with the sport . . . I got to live out a lot of dreams that most kids dream of since they were little kids in "Mommy and Me" classes.'[1]

Her dreams accelerated once she took up training full-time. The same year she left school, she won the all-around[ii] junior title at the American Classic in Huntsville, Texas, and the all-around junior title at the U.S. Classic in Chicago.[iii] A year later, she won the all-around title at the World Gymnastics Championships in Belgium. She went on to win the title the

'To do this sport, it does come with fear, but then you also have to be fearless. You have to be brave and trust in yourself.'

two following years, making her the first
woman to do so consecutively. Then it was on
to the 2016 Summer Olympic Games in Rio
de Janeiro in Brazil, where she dominated the
competition, walking away with five medals –
four gold and one bronze.[iv] Throughout it all,
she demonstrated determination and strength.

Perseverance aside, Simone has again
and again shown her extraordinary capacity
for kindness and joy. Known for her bubbly
personality she has openly encouraged her
competitors and celebrated their wins. She
has also stressed the importance of having
fun. Most athletes initially become involved in
sports because it interests them – and with
gymnast careers typically ending before thirty,
the ride is fleeting. 'It won't be for forever,
so enjoy the time that you have', she says.[2]
Despite her relentlessly positive attitude,
she does get nervous. There is an intense
pressure placed on athletes, especially those
competing on the global stage, and add to
that the expectations placed on someone who
has already proven themselves with multiple
achievements. To manage stress, Simone tries
to focus on herself and her goals, using her

headphones to tune out, and practicing deep breaths. 'I just try to stay calm, stay in the zone, listen to some music, and think of it one day at a time rather than it as a whole.'[3]

Not one to shy away from the truth, she is frank and open when it comes to the issues she cares about. When Russian hackers released personal medical records of a number of athletes, she used the opportunity to speak about living with Attention Deficit Hyperactivity Disorder (ADHD), declaring that she was not ashamed of taking medication for the condition. An advocate for gender equality, she has challenged the idea that women should downplay their successes. 'It's important to teach our female youth that it's okay to say, "Yes, I am good at this," and you don't hold back', she insists. 'You only see the men doing it. And they're praised for it and the women are looked down upon for it.'[4]

In 2018, Simone disclosed that she was one of more than a hundred female athletes sexually abused by Larry Nassar, the former team doctor for USA Gymnastics (USAG), the national governing body for gymnastics in the United States. Releasing a statement on the eve of his sentencing, she shared her struggle: 'I too am one of the many survivors that was sexually abused by Larry Nassar . . . There are many reasons that I have been reluctant to share my story, but I know now that it is not my fault'.[5] She publicly criticized USAG for failing to protect its young female athletes, demanding better. Nassar pleaded guilty to seven counts of sexual assault in January 2018 and was sentenced to 40–175 years in prison. The following month, he pleaded guilty to a further three counts of sexual assault, and was sentenced to an additional 40–125 years. After the sentencing, Simone published a celebratory tweet commending the survivors who had testified and offered her support. But the abuse that she and her fellow athletes were subjected to had a lasting impact. In 2019, she opened up and shared that she had sought professional help. 'I go to therapy to help with that because there were times when I didn't want to set foot in a gym', she revealed. 'But am I going to let that keep me from my passion, and the goals that I still have? It's just another bump you have to get over.'[6]

Proving that she would not let the experience define her, Simone competed intensively throughout 2018 and 2019. Over those two years she broke various records, most notably for the most women's all-around Gymnastics World Championship titles, and the most World medals won by a gymnast of any gender. It's a trend she hopes to continue, with the 2020 Summer Olympic Games[v] in Tokyo, Japan, in her sights. And as for what the future holds after the Games, a move away from gymnastics is on the cards. 'I'll be twenty-three, and for a gymnast that's pretty old. I mean, it's time to move', she explains. With her energy, drive and passion, the possibilities are endless. 'I've been in this sport. I've accomplished a lot. I think I need to see what else I can accomplish.'[7]

'There are always little steps that you have to get before you reach the bigger goal.'

The Interview

Tell us a bit about yourself, how you got into gymnastics and what your aspirations were at the beginning.

I'm Simone Biles, I'm twenty-two, and I'm a four-time Olympic gold medallist.

I was a very hyperactive kid, always bouncing all over the place. I got started in gymnastics from a day-care field trip; we were actually supposed to go to an oil ranch that day, but it got rained out so they took us to a gym down the street – Bannon's Gymnastix – which also happened to be where I first started when I was six. They saw the potential that I had and my muscular stature. They saw me copying some of the older girls in the back of the gym so they sent a letter home, and then that's how it all evolved.

As soon as I started I could do somersaults and backflips and backbends and leaps, and I would always just bounce off my butt too and stand up, which is unnatural, especially at that age. When I started out, I just wanted to have fun. I really didn't have any goals through the sport – it was the first time ever doing or learning about it – I just wanted to have fun and play around.

At what point did you become aware that
people were thinking, 'Maybe one day this kid
could actually be a world champion'?

I feel like, at six years old, a lot of people
believed in me before I believed in myself,
but I always thought it was only because
I was small, I was powerful, and I was
bouncing all over the place. So I didn't really
take it into consideration until I got to maybe
fourteen, fifteen, sixteen years old. That's
when I actually saw the potential in myself.

Did you have confidence early on?

I had a lot of pride and joy in doing
something I was good at, and then I thought,
'Okay, maybe I can go to college and do
this'. So my main goal was to get a college
scholarship. Here and there I had some
confidence, but you kind of go up and down
with those levels of confidence, especially
moving through the levels of gymnastics.

What were your aspirations as a kid?

When I was young I just wanted to do college gymnastics – I mean every gymnast wants to go to the Olympics, but then as you get older, you're like, 'Okay, the percentage and possibility is kind of slim'. I didn't realize that I had a shot until I was sixteen, seventeen, eighteen years old.

Now you've achieved everything that anyone could want to achieve in gymnastics, and more, what really matters to you?

There are a lot of things that matter to me in life and I still love what I do, but right now, what matters to me is teaching female youth that it's okay to be good at what you do, and it's also okay to speak up and believe in yourself. So I want to teach female youth empowerment because once you realize you're confident and good at something, it serves as positive reinforcement and empowers you to be even better.

There tends to be a lot of positive messaging for men, particularly as it relates

to confidence. A lot of the male athletes get
to say and prove and do their celebration
dances, and it's okay if they say they're good,
they tend to be praised for it. However, that
same messaging hasn't existed for women
and as soon as a female speaks up about it,
it's kind of frowned upon.

Why is that, do you think?

I think it has a little bit to do with sexism,
but at the end of the day I think people find
more joy in men succeeding than women
succeeding, because I think it terrifies men
if a woman is better than a male. It's just
the generation.

Do you have a particular aspiration or goal
beyond gymnastics?

I've been known to change my mind on this,
depending on the day! Who knows what the
future holds? I'm still pretty young and I feel
like there's still a long way to go, but my
gymnastics career will hopefully wrap up soon-
ish. In the long term, I am sure I will remain

active in the sport in some capacity, and I plan to continue to advocate for athlete/child safety in the future to help facilitate real change.

Then after that I want to be a voice for the voiceless and hopefully inspire foster kids. Everybody has it different, and you can't choose what circumstances you're born into, so I think speaking up for the voiceless is really important.

Tell us about your experience with foster care.

In my early years I was actually with my biological mom, and then we got taken from her and placed into foster care for a couple of years. Then my grandparents came and flew us down here to Texas. We stayed with them for a bit, but then we got put back in foster care, and a little bit after that we were officially adopted by my grandparents, who are now my parents. But we were very lucky with our foster care family and our situation, because most kids don't get to stay with their siblings, and we did – most kids get moved around a lot with their placements, and thankfully we only had to go to one foster care. So I just want to be a voice for them.

'It's hard mentally and physically.
I remember some of the days
I'm like: "Why am I here? What
am I doing? What did I do?"
But in the end it's all worth it.'

What does family mean to you? Your family has
built and runs the World Champions Centre, a
facility in Houston. What does that mean to you
beyond your own achievements?

I think family is the most important because,
at the end of the day, all you have is family,
and my parents have made a lot of sacrifices,
as well as my siblings, for me to be where
I am today. So I'm very, very grateful for them,
and one of the sacrifices they made was to
build this facility. Then we moved out here and
now it's home to a lot of gymnasts in the area,
so it's not just a home for me, but it's a home
for the community.

There're a lot of kids in the community
out here and it's not just a place where
I train – it was built for the community –
so I think people get that mistaken a lot in
that they think my parents built this gym
for me, Simone Biles, but it was just for
the community. My parents knew what it
was like whenever I was really high-energy,
and they wanted to place me into a safe
place. So we don't only have gymnastics,
but also Taekwondo, we have robotics,
we have a dance studio, and as well as

gymnastics we also have A&T [acrobatics and tumbling], T&T [trampoline and tumbling] and artistic programmes.

It's a family affair. My dad does help out – he's retired but he does help out with some of the stuff. My mom manages the whole place, my brother is the general manager of the building, and then my sister coaches and works at the front desk.

Everyone's family situation is different, and I feel like I've been very blessed my whole entire life to have such a tight-knit family and to grow up with them. Even now at twenty-two years old, we all live around each other, which is kinda cool because usually a family gets spread out all over, either the country or the state. So I'm definitely lucky and blessed to have them all right here in Houston.

What is your greatest happiness?

What brings me my greatest joy right now would probably be friends, family, making other people happy, doing what's right, no matter the circumstance, speaking up for what you believe in. I have a dog, food, pizza!

I feel like food makes everybody happy too. But I feel like whatever brings everybody together is what makes you happy. Yeah. I feel like a lot of things make me happy, honestly.

Do you still feel joy and satisfaction from your gymnastics, or is it starting to feel like pressure?

I feel like it's a good combination. I have a lot of pride and joy in what I do out here in the gym, but it's also still fun. That's why I still do it. Because if it felt more like a job or too much pressure, I feel like I would have given it up already, and I haven't.

What do you regard as the lowest depth of misery?

For me I feel like it would be the loss of all hope; hope in and out of the gym, and in whatever you do. Because I feel like once your confidence drops, then you just get really sad and depressed and you don't believe in yourself as much as other people believe in you. And I think that's really hard to continue through life and whatever you're doing at that moment. I feel like it [self-belief]

makes you a better person and it brings
out your confidence.

I am a positive person, so I always try
to find some good in all things, even in the
most difficult of circumstances. Oftentimes
that's easier said than done, even for me
right now, but I remain hopeful that change is
possible, and circumstances do not have to be
permanent. I feel that there is finally a crack in
the system where women's rights matter and
abuse of any kind should not be tolerated and
accepted. I feel that speaking out is becoming
the norm and no one should feel afraid to use
their voice. I am disappointed that we are
even having to have this conversation, but
sadly we see this type of behaviour across all
industries. It's wrong and it's unacceptable.

Can you describe a key moment or crisis which
has profoundly influenced you or your life?

I believe everything happens for a reason, and
my reason was to do gymnastics, and I feel like
I would have never been put in this position if
I wasn't adopted by my grandparents. So I feel
like that's probably the biggest thing.

I believe that our life is shaped by all of our collective moments – good, bad and everything in between. Each moment does have an impact, whether you realize it at the time or not, and to what extent it can change over time. My experience with foster care. We do not pick the circumstances we are born into, but they do not have to define you or your life's journey.

Do you have guiding principles or a driving philosophy that underpins your life and decisions?

My mom always told me since I was a very young girl, 'to be the best Simone', and that is a guiding principle that has really worked for me. She reminds me of this all the time, and I love her for it. And it doesn't matter what I do, I fall back on that quote. Just because it's a hard day, everybody has hard days, so you can't give up. So I always try to tell myself 'to be the best Simone', because there's always going to be little kids looking up to me and watching whatever I do, whether that's in or out of the gym. So I try to be the best person for myself, and I think that inspires other people. And myself.

Despite what people may think, it's not always about winning for me. Sometimes it could be, but for me it's hitting the best sets I can, gaining confidence and having a good time and having fun. If you're having fun, that's when the best memories are built.

What does 'being the best Simone' entail?

It would be to be a good person, be a good athlete, always put one hundred per cent effort in whatever I do. Whether that's school, gym, any of my sponsorships that I have, representing the country whenever I go out to compete, I think you should always try to be the best version of yourself.

Also, never give up, no matter what the circumstance.

Your mother taught you goal-setting at a young age?

Yes. Very. At the beginning of every year she would have me and my sister come into the

'To go out there and prove what
I can do has taught me a lot
about who I am. We can push
ourselves further. We always
have more to give.'

office with a notebook and write down three short-term goals, three long-term goals; however many your list is, it doesn't really matter. I mean it's worked all these years, so I can't complain!

How old were you when you did that for the first time?

Oh goodness, we were young! I was still in grade school. She wouldn't let us leave until we had our goals written down. And there were times as I got older where I wanted to be stubborn and I wanted to keep the goals to myself, but I felt like saying it out loud and putting it on paper really makes you want to go for it, and sets you up to start.

Each year we still have to do it. So don't go too high, but if it's a long-term goal then you can still put it on for the next year.

So your mother has had a big influence on you?

Yes, both of my parents have. They've always taught me to do everything one hundred per cent; always be kind to people because it's a reflection of you, how you've been brought up; and they've always taught us to never give up; to always have fun in what we do, and if you are not having fun, then don't do it, because there's no point in putting fifty per cent effort into something. So I think that's why my siblings and I have been successful in whatever we've done throughout the years.

Because both of my parents came from very different backgrounds [than us], and so they've always set us up to have the best, most successful life that we can have, because their childhoods weren't easy. And so they want to set us up for success.

What do you think were the things that led them on a path of being inspirational themselves?

I think everybody wants to be great at something, so as soon as you start and you put your first step forward, you just start [down] that path and you don't give up until you're successful and you're happy with where you're at: living situation, moneywise, mental, physical, health. And I think that helps.

They've always taught us to give back,
because we've had so much given to us.
And if you give back, you get back.

What qualities have been most critical to achieving
goals during your life and career?

I think believing in yourself, being confident, not
giving up, giving one hundred per cent effort in
whatever you do. I think there's a lot. I mean,
it's not easy to do gymnastics, and I feel like
you grow qualities as you get older, and you
mature and you learn through the sport.

What are the daily disciplines and routines
you practice?

My daily routine is I train six or seven hours a day.
I start at eight, so my first practice is from eight
to eleven-thirty, and then my second practice
starts at three, and I usually go to five-thirty, six
or just whenever I finish for the night. And I do
that Monday through Friday, and then Saturday is
eight to twelve. And then we have Sundays off.
    It's definitely exhausting, but you have to
remember the reasons why you're doing it.

And I think that really helps me on those hard days to not give up, because I know what the end outcome is and the goal that I have set for myself, and what I want to do. So I think that's always what's helped me keep pushing and not give up, is the goals I have set for myself.

Now that I've gotten older and I've matured, I've had to take care of my body a lot more than if I was thirteen, fourteen, and so I do a lot of rehab and therapies so that my body recuperates for the next day, but I do wake up with aches and pains. But if you ask any elite athlete, they are in pain in some shape or form.

How do you overcome challenges?

There are days when I think I can't do it, but, you know, I always take everything one step at a time. One day at a time. One workout at a time. Because that really helps me get through it. Because if I think, 'Oh my gosh, it's a month before I have a break, or this or that', then I get wrapped up in my head and I won't want to do it. So I like to take everything day by day.

My mom has always told me that although I am small, that doesn't limit my power or define me. So I don't think about size; I focus my energy on being powerful and confident. I think we can push ourselves further than we think; we have more to give than we realize. At the end of the day, I'd rather regret the risks that didn't work out, than the chances I didn't take at all.

Sometimes if I – I wouldn't say if I have failures, but if I have setbacks – I go back to the drawing board and I reroute it, see what I can do different to best set myself up for success. But I feel like everybody needs some time to decompress, and you should give yourself one day to just be sad about it, and then you pick yourself up and you keep going.

Just one day?

One day. Because it if lasts for more than one day then it's too much, you kind of blew it.

You've proven to yourself that you can
push through?

Most definitely. I feel like I've pushed through
a lot of things, and I've overcome a lot of
injuries, self-doubt, problems in the gym.

Do you think courage has been an important
part of your success?

Yes, I think so. But to start in the sport of
gymnastics, you have to be courageous
because it's not an easy sport. But you can
excel pretty quickly, and that's when it gets
scary and a little bit more dangerous, and you
have to defy gravity a little bit more, so yes.

You talk about 'defying gravity'. Is this
something you've taught yourself?

I feel like my air-awareness has been really
good since I've been a kid, but it's definitely
something that you have to work on, and
that's why we use the trampolines and the
pits so that we have better self-awareness and
the air-awareness to know exactly where your
body is at all times. So that you're safe.

'I'd rather regret the risks that
didn't work out than the chances
I didn't take at all.'

Are there moments of utter elation when you
achieve a new goal you've set yourself?

Most definitely, yes. I am very elated
whenever I land a skill, or I perform a new skill
and it gets named after me, or it's something
that nobody's ever done before.

But you're able to stay grounded?

Yes. My family has taught me to be
humble, because you always have to work
for what you get, and at the end of the day
you are just the same person like everybody
else around you. You're normal.

So, six-year-olds around the world can become
as successful as you are?

Yes!

What does leadership mean to you?

Besides being the best version of yourself in
whatever you do, it means being kind. I feel
like no matter the circumstances, kids will

be looking up to you, so you have to be the best version of yourself in whatever you do. Because in the gym I have all these kids looking up to me, so I try to be the best version of myself so that one day they will want to do the same.

Leadership, to me, means having courage to do the right thing, speaking up for what you believe in, no matter the consequences, and always doing the right thing. We are all human and nobody's perfect, but it shouldn't be that hard to treat people fairly and respectfully. And if you make a mistake or do something wrong, take responsibility for your actions. Actions speak louder than words.

There have been moments in your life when you've had to speak up and do the right thing?

Yes. I feel like I have the privilege. I was given the privilege to have a platform, so I need to use that in a positive manner. And I feel like I have done that over the past couple of years, especially being more outspoken as I've gotten older and being a voice for the voiceless.

You had the courage of your convictions to
stand up for the other women in relation
to Larry Nassar?

Well, for me it's hard to speak up about some
of those things, but I did it because I knew it
would help other women speak up and come
forward, and it would help them. And it also
did help me get that burden off my chest, but
I knew it would help a lot of other people out
there, men and women.

I think the truth sets you free, but you
also have to do what's right.

Has there been a special individual or individuals
that have particularly inspired you by their
example or wisdom?

My mom and dad! Their love and support
keeps me grounded but also gives me the
courage to pursue my dreams. As I get older,
I have a better understanding and appreciation
for their strength and the foundation they have
blessed me with through their unconditional
love and support.

A lot of the [other] powerful leaders,
the people who I look up to, have a lot of

confidence in whatever they do, because I feel like once you're confident you're better at what you do. So again, it's saying, 'Yes, I'm good at this and it's okay to say I'm good at this'.

What do you think the world needs more of now?

I feel like the world needs more empathy. Everybody's so quick to judge, everyone's 'normal' is not the same. We need to be more compassionate and empathetic with one another, we just have to let it happen, especially with today's generation, the youth. Everybody's really quick to judge everyone's situation, when behind closed doors you have no idea what's going on or happening. We have to judge less.

If you could change anything in the world, what would you change?

Equality. Equality for all people, because I feel like everybody should be looked at equally, no matter religion, race, male or female, gender. So I'd really like to see that change, but obviously it's going to take a while and history repeats itself.

Yes. I feel like there're a lot more women leaders in today's generation and it's exciting to see. If you ask kids who it is, they'll start naming females, and it just shows you times are changing and coming around.

I will say female leaders as well – I really love Michelle Obama and Serena Williams. I think Michelle would have been an amazing president – I wish they could have shared their time, she and Obama. She always speaks up for the voiceless; I think she's very confident in whatever she wants to do; I think she helps people in times that they have lost hope. She really stands for what she believes in, and I think that's really important, especially to be so open about it.

And I love how dominant Serena is; she speaks up for what she believes in too. She's powerful, she has a lot of strength, and she proves that no matter the circumstances you can still go out and win. Because she's had a kid and she's had other things happen to her, she's also taught me to not give up.

What is your hope for your generation?

My hope is to inspire kids everywhere to know that you can do anything you put your mind to. Dream big, work hard, put your best foot forward, take calculated risks, and just never give up. Do it for yourself, and make sure to keep it fun!

If you were to choose one word of all words that you most identify with, that's at the heart of who you are, what would that single word be?

Confident!

'Every gold-medal winning performance is a highlight, but sometimes I like to think of the things that made me better as a person. It's those times where I didn't go out and do my best, but it still went okay in the end.'

About Simone Biles

Simone Biles is a twenty-three-year-old American artistic gymnast, and is one of the most decorated gymnasts of all time. Born in Columbus, Ohio, in 1997, her family environment was challenging as she and her younger sister spent time in foster care until they were legally adopted by their grandparents. When she was six, Biles visited a local gym during a day care field trip. The gymnastics instructors suggested she pursue the sport, so she enrolled in classes and began training with coach Aimee Boorman two years later.

With Boorman's support and guidance, Biles excelled at junior competitions. In 2011, she began her elite career at the American Classic in Houston, where she placed third all-around. Realizing her potential, she left high school in favour of being home-schooled, which enabled her to increase her training from twenty to upwards of thirty hours a week. The decision paid off; she made the U.S. Junior National team in 2012 and the following year had her senior international debut at the American Cup,[vi] where she finished second. After a couple of disappointing performances later in the year, she went on to take the title of national all-around champion at the 2013 USA Gymnastics National Championships. This led to her being named to the Senior National Team, and eventually the World Gymnastics Championships (WGC) team.

In October 2013, Biles competed in her first WGC in Belgium and won the individual women's all-around, becoming the first African American to do so. Her success continued into 2014 and 2015, when she again won the world all-around title – becoming the first woman to win three consecutive all-around titles in WGC history. She qualified for the 2016 U.S. Olympic Team and competed in the Summer Olympic Games in Rio de Janeiro where she won her first Olympic medal in the team event, followed by medals in the individual all-around, individual vault and women's floor. With a total of four Olympic gold medals and one bronze, she set a U.S. record for the most won in women's gymnastics at a single Olympic Games.

Biles's autobiography, *Courage to Soar: A Body in Motion, A Life in Balance* written with journalist Michelle Burford, was published in 2016 and reached number one on *The New York Times* Young Adult bestsellers list. Shortly after competing in season twenty-four of *Dancing with the Stars* (where she finished fourth), she made her return to gymnastics to compete at the 2018 WGC in Doha, Qatar. Despite suffering from a kidney stone – and being unable to take painkillers because of anti-doping regulations – she won the floor, vault, and team and individual all-arounds, and placed third in the balance beam.

Continuing her success into 2018 and 2019, Biles has been touted as redefining gymnastics with her confidence, strength, focus and accuracy. There are several moves named after her, including the 'double-double' beam dismount (two twists with two flips). She has won nineteen World titles, and has won the most gold medals at a single Olympics, taking home four at Rio de Janeiro in 2016. In 2019 she set a new record when she became the first woman to win five all-around titles at the WGC, and the first woman to land a triple-double on her floor routine. At the time of printing, she has a total of twenty-five World medals, making her the gymnast with the most World medals of any gender.

@simonebiles

About the Project

'A true leader must work hard to ease tensions, especially when dealing with sensitive and complicated issues. Extremists normally thrive when there is tension, and pure emotion tends to supersede rational thinking.'

– Nelson Mandela

Inspired by Nelson Mandela, *I Know This to Be True* was conceived to record and share what really matters for the most inspiring leaders of our time.

I Know This to Be True is a Nelson Mandela Foundation project anchored by original interviews with twelve different and extraordinary leaders each year, for five years – six men and six women – who are helping and inspiring others through their ideas, values and work.

Royalties from sales of this book will support language translation and free access to films, books and educational programmes using material from the series, in all countries with developing economies, or economies in transition, as defined by United Nations annual classifications.

iknowthistobetrue.org

'A good head and a good
heart are always a formidable
combination.'

– Nelson Mandela

A special thanks to Simone Biles, and all the generous and inspiring individuals we call leaders who have magnanimously given their time to be part of this project.

For the Nelson Mandela Foundation:
Sello Hatang, Verne Harris, Noreen Wahome, Razia Saleh and Sahm Venter

For Blackwell & Ruth:
Geoff Blackwell, Ruth Hobday, Cameron Gibb, Nikki Addison, Olivia van Velthooven, Elizabeth Blackwell, Kate Raven, Annie Cai and Tony Coombe

We hope that together we can help to mobilize Madiba's extraordinary legacy, to the benefit of communities around the world.

A note from the photographer

The photographic portraits in this book are the result of a team effort, led by Blackwell & Ruth's talented design director Cameron Gibb. I would also like to acknowledge the on-the-ground support of Matty Wong for helping me capture these images of Simone Biles.

– Geoff Blackwell

About Nelson Mandela

Nelson Mandela was born in the Transkei, South Africa, on 18 July 1918. He joined the African National Congress in the early 1940s and was engaged in struggles against the ruling National Party's apartheid system for many years before being arrested in August 1962. Mandela was incarcerated for more than twenty-seven years, during which his reputation as a potent symbol of resistance for the anti-apartheid movement grew steadily. Released from prison in 1990, Mandela was jointly awarded the Nobel Peace Prize in 1993, and became South Africa's first democratically elected president in 1994. He died on 5 December 2013, at the age of ninety-five.

N E L S O N   M A N D E L A
F O U N D A T I O N

Living the legacy

About the Nelson Mandela Foundation

The Nelson Mandela Foundation is a non-profit organization founded by Nelson Mandela in 1999 as his post-presidential office. In 2007 he gave it a mandate to promote social justice through dialogue and memory work.

Its mission is to contribute to the making of a just society by mobilizing the legacy of Nelson Mandela, providing public access to information on his life and times and convening dialogue on critical social issues.

The Foundation strives to weave leadership development into all aspects of its work.

nelsonmandela.org

Notes

i   As at the time of publication, Biles is a five-time World Artistic
    Gymnastics Championship all-around champion (2013–15, 2018–19),
    a six-time U.S. national all-around champion (2013–16, 2018–19),
    a member of four gold-medal-winning U.S. teams at the World
    Artistic Gymnastics Championships (2014–15, 2018–2019), and
    the most decorated U.S. gymnast (and third most decorated
    gymnast worldwide) of all time.

ii A gymnastics term which refers to a single athlete
    competing across all gymnastics apparatus in their gender
    competition category (four for women; six for men).

iii The American Classic and the U.S. Classic are annual summer
    gymnastics meets for U.S. elite female artistic gymnasts
    and serve as the two qualifiers to the USA Gymnastics
    National Championships.

iv Biles won gold medals for the individual all-around event,
    women's vault, women's floor exercise and the gymnastics
    team event, and bronze for women's balance beam.

v   The 2020 Summer Olympic Games were postponed due to the
    COVID-19 pandemic and will take place in 2021. The event will keep
    the name 'Tokyo 2020' for marketing and branding purposes.

vi The American Cup is an elite senior level international gymnastics
    competition held in the U.S. in February or March of each year,
    and is part of the International Federation of Gymnastics (FIG)
    Artistic Gymnastics World Cup series.

Sources and Permissions

1   "Simone Biles: The Courage to Soar", Academy of Achievement,
        18 October 2017, achievement.org/achiever/simone-biles/#interview.
2   Trupti Rami, "Simone Biles Is Back", papermag.com, papermag.com/
        simone-biles-sports-2580082511.
3   Ibid.
4   Nancy Armour, "Simone Biles on where she keeps all those medals,
        her favorite athletes, her future", USA Today, 12 October 2019,
        usatoday.com/story/sports/2019/10/12/simone-biles-her-legacy-and-
        future-after-tokyo-olympics/3946156002.
5   Simone Biles, 'Most of you know me as a happy, giggly, and energetic girl',
        Twitter, 15 January 2018, twitter.com/Simone_Biles/status/953014513837715457.
6   Emma Brockes, "Simone Biles: 'I go to therapy, because at times I didn't
        want to set foot in the gym'", The Guardian, 16 March 2019, theguardian.com/
        sport/2019/mar/16/simone-biles-therapy-times-didnt-want-set-foot-gym.
7   Trupti Rami, "Simone Biles Is Back", papermag.com, papermag.com/
        simone-biles-sports-2580082511.

The publisher is grateful for literary permissions to reproduce items
subject to copyright which have been used with permission. Every effort
has been made to trace the copyright holders and the publisher apologizes
for any unintentional omission. We would be pleased to hear from any
not acknowledged here and undertake to make all reasonable efforts to
include the appropriate acknowledgement in any subsequent edition.

Page 6: Gabrielle McMillen, "Rio Olympics 2016: Simone Biles cements golden
legacy: 'I've finally done it'", Sporting News, 8 December 2016, sportingnews.com/us/
athletics/news/rio-olympics-2016-simone-biles-all-around-gold-individual-medal-final-fiv
e/1x4a8qszafv001jb5bjtn3i90q; pages 13–14, 20: "Simone Biles: The Courage to Soar",
Academy of Achievement, 18 October 2017, achievement.org; pages 16–17, 19: "Simone
Biles Is Back", Trupti Rami, PAPER magazine, Summer 2018, papermag.com/simone-
biles-sports-2580082511; pages 17–18, 57: Nancy Armour, "Simone Biles on where
she keeps all those medals, her favorite athletes, her future", USA Today, 12 October
2019, usatoday.com/story/sports/2019/10/12/simone-biles-her-legacy-and-future-after-
tokyo-olympics/3946156002; page 18: Simone Biles, "Most of you know me as a
happy, giggly, and energetic girl", Twitter, 15 January 2018, twitter.com/Simone_Biles/
status/953014513837715457; pages 19, 30: Emma Brockes, "Simone Biles: 'I go to
therapy, because at times I didn't want to set foot in the gym'", The Guardian, 16 March
2019, theguardian.com/sport/2019/mar/16/simone-biles- therapy-times-didnt-want-set-
foot-gym; page 38: Sade Strehlke, "How August Cover Star Simone Biles Blazes Through
Expectations", Teen Vogue, copyright © Condé Nast, 30 June 2016, teenvogue.com/story/
simone-biles-summer-olympics-cover-august-2016; page 49: Simone Biles, "I'd rather regret
the risks", Twitter, 10 May 2016, twitter.com/Simone_Biles/status/730255395554365441;
pages 65–66: Nelson Mandela by Himself: The Authorised Book of Quotations edited
by Sello Hatang and Sahm Venter (Johannesburg, South Africa: Pan Macmillan, 2017),
copyright © 2011 Nelson R. Mandela and the Nelson Mandela Foundation, used by
permission of the Nelson Mandela Foundation, Johannesburg, South Africa.

First published in the United States of America in 2020 by Chronicle Books LLC.

Produced and originated by
Blackwell and Ruth Limited
Suite 405, Ironbank, 150 Karangahape Road
Auckland 1010, New Zealand
www.blackwellandruth.com

Publisher: Geoff Blackwell
Editor in Chief & Project Editor: Ruth Hobday
Design Director: Cameron Gibb
Designer & Production Coordinator: Olivia van Velthooven
Publishing Manager: Nikki Addison
Digital Publishing Manager: Elizabeth Blackwell

Library of Congress Cataloging-in-Publication Data available.

ISBN 978-1-7972-0022-4

Chronicle Books LLC
680 Second Street
San Francisco, CA 94107
www.chroniclebooks.com

10 9 8 7 6 5 4 3 2 1

Manufactured in China by 1010 Printing Ltd.